DAVID BOWIE

Anthology

HAL LEONARD
PUBLISHING
CORPORATION

Home Office: National Sales Office:
960 East Mark Street 8112 West Bluemound Road
Winona MN 55987   Milwaukee WI 53213

DAVID BOWIE *Anthology*

Alphabetical Contents

Chronological Listing
Record Album - Year - Songs

The Laughing Gnome

Words and Music by
DAVID BOWIE

6

8

Cygnet Committee

Words and Music by
DAVID BOWIE

Sound And Vision

Words and Music by
DAVID BOWIE

Space Oddity

Words and Music by
DAVID BOWIE

Moderately slow

The Bewlay Brothers

Words and Music by
DAVID BOWIE

Changes

Words and Music by
DAVID BOWIE

40

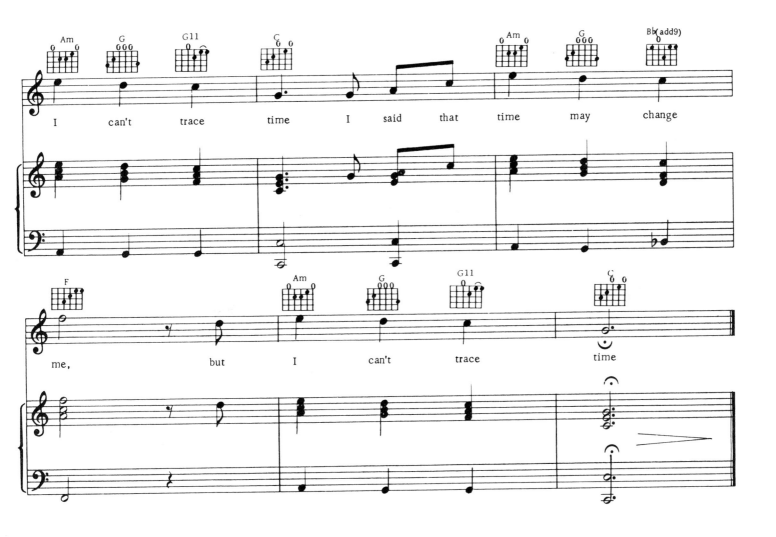

Verse 2.

I watch the ripples change their size, but never leave the stream
Of warm impermanence and so the days flow thru my eyes
But still the days seem the same.
And these children that you spit on as they try to change their worlds
Are immune to your consultations, they're quite aware of what they're going thru'

(Chorus 2.)

(Ch-ch-ch-ch-Changes) Turn and face the stranger -
(Ch-ch-changes) Don't tell them to grow up and out of it,
(Ch-ch-ch-ch-changes) Turn and face the stranger
(Ch-ch-changes) where's your shame, you've left us up to our necks in it
Time may change me, but you can't trace time.   (To Interlude)

Life On Mars

Words and Music by
DAVID BOWIE

46

Queen Bitch

Words and Music by
DAVID BOWIE

53

56

Quicksand

Words and Music by
DAVID BOWIE

All The Madmen

Words & Music by
DAVID BOWIE

(Spoken) Where can the horizon lie when a nation hides it's organic minds in a cellar dark and grim they must be

D.S. al Coda

very dim.

CODA

Zane, zane, zane,___ ou - vre le chien.___

repeat and fade

Zane, zane, zane,___ ou - vre le chien.___

Supermen

Words and Music by
DAVID BOWIE

The Man Who Sold The World

Words and Music by
DAVID BOWIE

Rock 'N' Roll Suicide

Words and Music by
DAVID BOWIE

84

Soul Love

Words and Music by
DAVID BOWIE

Suffragette City

Words and Music by
DAVID BOWIE

92

Ziggy Stardust

Words and Music by
DAVID BOWIE

95

Starman

Words and Music by
DAVID BOWIE

John, I'm Only Dancing

Words and Music by
DAVID BOWIE

wrong _____ I'm on-ly danc - ing _____

danc - ing _____

To Coda ⊕

D. S. al Coda

⊕ CODA

4 times

4 times

Drive-In Saturday

Words and Music by
DAVID BOWIE

106

The Jean Genie

Words and Music by
DAVID BOWIE

Diamond Dogs

Words and Music by
DAVID BOWIE

Rebel Rebel

Words and Music by
DAVID BOWIE

Do do do do___ do do do do

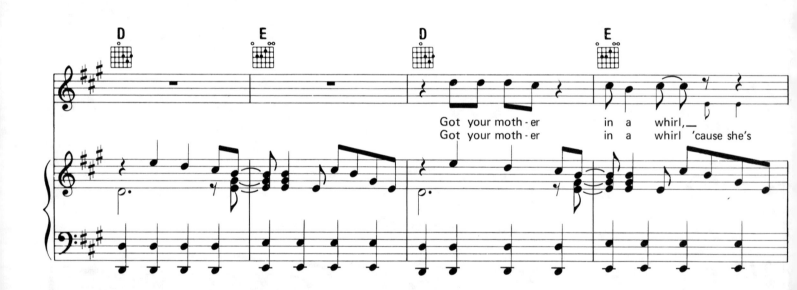

Got your moth - er   in a   whirl,___
Got your moth - er   in a   whirl 'cause she's

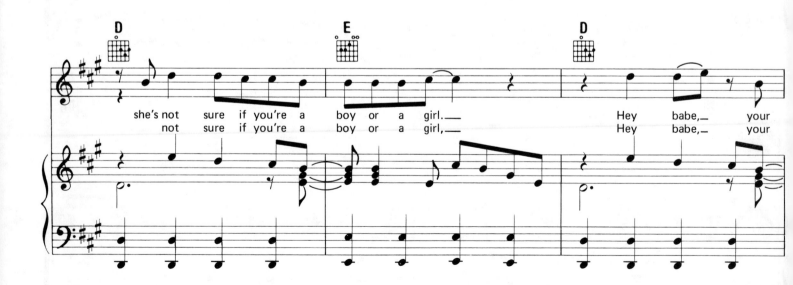

she's not   sure if you're a   boy or a   girl.___   Hey   babe,___   your
not   sure if you're a   boy or a   girl,___   Hey   babe,___   your

115

TVC 15

Words and Music by
DAVID BOWIE

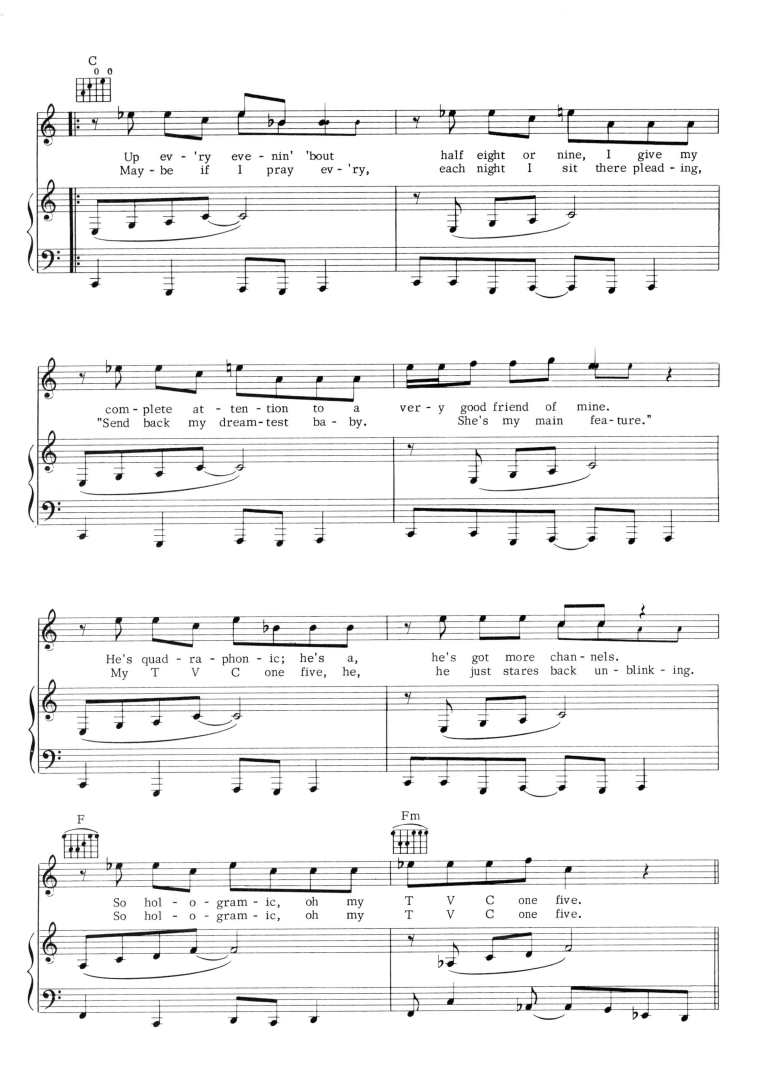

Fame

Words and Music by DAVID BOWIE,
JOHN LENNON and CARLOS ALOMAR

1. Fame makes a man take things o-ver. Fame lets him
2. Fame, what you like is in the li-mo. Fame, what you

loose, hard to swal-low. Fame puts you there where things are hol-low,
get is no to-mor-row. Fame, what you need you have to bor-row,

Young Americans

Words and Music by
DAVID BOWIE

With a heavy beat (in 2)

They pulled in just be - hind the fridge,— he lays her down.— He frowns,—

"Gee, my life's a fun - ny thing. Am I____ still too young?"

133

Golden Years

Words and Music by
DAVID BOWIE

Heroes

Words by DAVID BOWIE
Music by DAVID BOWIE and BRIAN ENO

I will be king.____
I will be king.____
And you,____
And you,____

144

beat them

for - ev - er and ev - er.

Oh, we can be he-

ly - ing;

then you bet -ter not stay.__

But we could be saf-

- roes

- er

just for one day. _____

just for one day. _____

D.S. and fade

Breaking Glass

Words by DAVID BOWIE
Music by DAVID BOWIE, DENNIS DAVIS
and GEORGE MURRAY

151

I'll nev-er touch you.

Repeat and fade
A

Repeat and fade

E

Boys Keep Swinging

Words by DAVID BOWIE
Music by DAVID BOWIE and BRIAN ENO

v'rite things when you're a boy. _____
when you're a boy. _____

Boys,

boys,

1. 2.

D. C. (instrumental) and fade

boys keep swing-ing. Boys al-ways work it out. Boys al-ways work it out.

Memory Of A Free Festival

Words and Music by
DAVID BOWIE

158

Ashes To Ashes

Words and Music by
DAVID BOWIE

Fashion

Words and Music by
DAVID BOWIE

Medium Slow Rock

168

Scary Monsters And Super Creeps

Words and Music by
DAVID BOWIE

Under Pressure

Words and Music by Freddie Mercury,
John Deacon, Brian May,
Roger Taylor and David Bowie

179

Cat People
(Putting Out Fire)

Music by GIORGIO MORODER
Words by DAVID BOWIE

China Girl

Words and Music by DAVID BOWIE
and IGGY POP

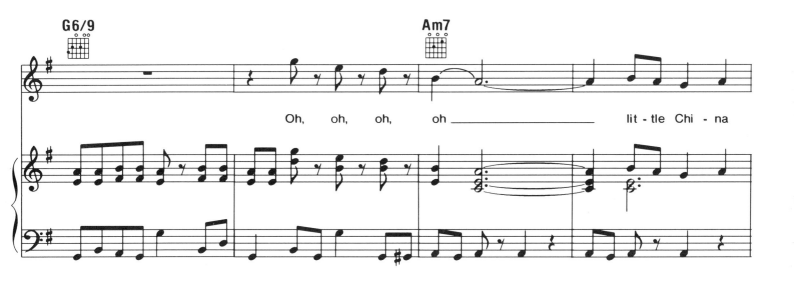

Oh, oh, oh, oh _____ lit-tle Chi-na

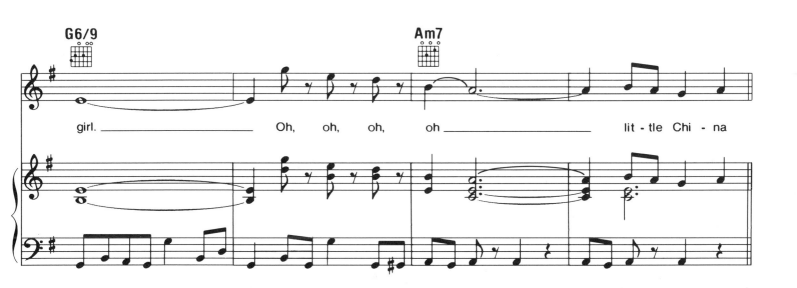

girl. _____ Oh, oh, oh, oh _____ lit-tle Chi-na

190

Let's Dance

Words and Music by
DAVID BOWIE

Modern Love

Words and Music by
DAVID BOWIE

Fast, Driving Rock

1. I catch a pa - per boy but it's
2. There's no sign of life it's
3. *(Third verse instrumental)*

4. It's not really work
   It's just the pow'r to charm
   Still standin' in the wind
   But I never wave bye bye
   But I try
   I try
   (Chorus)

Without You

Words and Music by
DAVID BOWIE

Gently, with a beat

Blue Jean

Words and Music by
DAVID BOWIE

Blue Jean,   I just met a girl named Blue _
One day   I'm gon-na write a po-em in a

_ Jean.   Blue Jean,   she's got a cam-ou-flaged face and no mon-
let - ter.   One day   I'm gon-na get that fac-ul-ty to-

ey.   Re - mem-ber,   they al-ways let you down when you
geth - er.   Re - mem-ber,   like ev'-ry-bod-y has to wait in

Tonight

Words and Music by
DAVID BOWIE and IGGY POP

Eve - ry-thing___ will be al - right___ To - night
Eve - ry-one___ will be al - right___ To-night

Eve - ry-thing___ will be al - right___ To - night
Eve - ry-one___ will be al - right___ To-night

214